Decorate Your Tree for Jesus

PALMETTO
PUBLISHING
Charleston, SC
www.PalmettoPublishing.com

Copyright © 2024 by Dee Ann Murphy

All rights reserved

No portion of this book may be reproduced, stored in a retrieval system, or transmitted in any form by any means—electronic, mechanical, photocopy, recording, or other—except for brief quotations in printed reviews, without prior permission of the author.

Hardcover ISBN: 9798822960077
Paperback ISBN: 9798822960084

Decorate Your Tree for Jesus

by Dee Ann Murphy

Illustrated by Brayden Curry

I wanted to share a tradition

with you that we have done for over 20 years. It all started by attending a women's conference and listening to someone speak about ways to make family traditions in the home. I liked some ideas that were shared and when my girls were young, we made our ornaments for the tree; macaroni angels, clothespin soldiers, and hand stuffed stars adorned our tree. This transformed into me writing the story on a notebook and eventually adapting this to a children's story.

The first time we invited others with small children to participate, it was a little chaotic. But we shared the gospel and it was fun for the kids. The decorating party has continued and the story proofed and changed several times. We had snacks, a hot chocolate bar, and decorated Christmas cookies before moving to the story. As the story was read, each designated ornament was placed on the tree. Each time I look at the tree, it reminds me of the Christmas story. I hope it will your family as well.

Christmas is a celebration of Jesus' birthday. God sent us His son as a little baby. Jesus would grow up to be a man without any sin. God wants us to live our life like Jesus.

Did you know our tree tells the story of Jesus' birth? The lighted Christmas tree reminds us of the starlit heavens from which Jesus came. The tree points to heaven, just like a tip of an arrow.

John 6:38

Our tree top angel is Gabriel. God sent the angel Gabriel to tell Mary that she was to have God's son. Mary was engaged to Joseph. When Mary told Joseph what had happened, he was worried about what to do. God told Joseph in a dream to go ahead and marry her for the child was the Son of God. Mary and Joseph did marry, and they lived in Nazareth. Joseph worked there as a carpenter.

Luke 1:26-38 Matthew 1:20, 21

The soldiers on our tree remind us of the government decree that required Mary and Joseph to travel to Bethlehem. Caesar Augustus ordered all people to return to their city of origin for a census. So, Mary and Joseph went to Bethlehem, the city of David. Joseph was from the family of David, and it was a long journey. Can you imagine riding on a donkey for 75 miles? That is about how far it was. Mary was pregnant. By the time they reached Bethlehem, she was very tired.

Luke 2:1-5

The city was so crowded with people for the census that they couldn't find a place to stay. They had to stay in a cave where they kept the animals. Mary gave birth to Jesus there and wrapped Him in cloth and laid Him in a manger. A manger is where they fed their animals. What a humble beginning for God's son, a King! The sheep on our tree should remind us where Jesus was born.

Luke 2:6,7

All those angels on the tree are singing. Can you hear them? They are praising God for they knew what a wonderful thing God had done. One angel was sent to tell the shepherds about the Christ child. He told them where to find Jesus. The shepherds were tending their flocks, and the angel appeared to them and told them the good news. Many angels appeared and started singing and praising God saying, "Glory to God in the highest, and on earth peace among men with whom He is pleased."

Luke 2:8-14

After the angels had gone, the shepherds hurried to see the Christ child. And after they had seen the things that the Lord had shown them, they told others about the baby. The shepherd's staffs are like the candy canes on our tree. The shepherds were the first to worship Jesus.

Luke 2:15-18

Later, the magi, who were wise men that studied the stars, had seen the great star in the East. The wicked king named Herod, had also heard about the baby. He wanted to destroy this child Jesus before he could become king. He told the magi to follow the star and find the child. He wanted them to report back to him after they had found Him. Well, the magi followed that bright star to Bethlehem and found the child, Jesus. We have many stars on our tree.

Matthew 2:9,10

There they worshipped Jesus and brought Him gifts fit for a king; gold, frankincense, and myrrh. The gold on our tree is fit for a king! God warned the magi in a dream not to report back to the evil King Herod. They left Bethlehem and returned to their own countries.

Luke 2:7-12

Jesus grew and taught all the people about who He was and how God loved them. He performed great miracles for them and tried to get them to live the way that God wanted. Jesus knew the reason He had come to earth. He knew that we all have sin in our hearts, just like the center of every snowflake begins with a speck of dirt. Romans 3:23 tells us that all have sinned. We cannot be holy and pure, no matter how good we are.

The Bible teaches us that Jesus paid the price for our sins. If we believe in Jesus, we are forgiven. The red berries on the holly branches in the tree should remind us of God's plan to save us. God loved us so much; He gave us His son. In John 3:16, it says, "For God so loved the world that He gave us His one and only son, that whoever believes in Him should not perish, but have eternal life." What a wonderful gift God gave us!

Merry Christmas

Milton Keynes UK
Ingram Content Group UK Ltd.
UKHW050708141024
449707UK00002B/21